History Raiders

Mysterious Disappearances

Cynthia O'Brien

CRABTREE
PUBLISHING COMPANY
WWW.CRABTREEBOOKS.COM

T0020817

Author: Cynthia O'Brien
Editors: Sarah Eason, Jennifer Sanderson, and Janine Deschenes
Proofreader and indexer: Tracey Kelly
Proofreader: Crystal Sikkens
Editorial director: Kathy Middleton
Design: Jessica Moon
Cover design: Katherine Berti
Photo research: Rachel Blount
Prepress and print coordination:
    Katherine Berti
Consultant: Rupert Matthews

Written, developed, and produced by Calcium

Library and Archives Canada Cataloguing in Publication

Title: Mysterious disappearances / Cynthia O'Brien.
Names: O'Brien, Cynthia (Cynthia J.), author.
Description: Series statement: History raiders |
    Includes bibliographical references and index.
Identifiers: Canadiana (print) 20210192550 |
    Canadiana (ebook) 20210192569 |
    ISBN 9781427151070 (hardcover) |
    ISBN 9781427151131 (softcover) |
    ISBN 9781427151193 (HTML) |
    ISBN 9781427151254 (EPUB)
Subjects: LCSH: Missing persons—Juvenile literature. |
    LCSH: Curiosities and wonders—Juvenile literature.
Classification: LCC AG244 .O27 2022 | DDC j001.94—dc23

Library of Congress Cataloging-in-Publication Data

Available at the Library of Congress

Crabtree Publishing Company

www.crabtreebooks.com   1-800-387-7650

Published in Canada
Crabtree Publishing
616 Welland Ave.
St. Catharines, Ontario
L2M 5V6

Published in the United States
Crabtree Publishing
347 Fifth Ave
Suite 1402-145
New York, NY 10016

Printed in the U.S.A./062021/CG20210401

CONTENTS

Vanishing Acts 4

Lost in Ancient Egypt 6

History Raider! The Lost Queen 8

A Roman Mystery 10

History Raider! Rome's Lost Legion 12

Medieval Murder? 14

History Raider! Princes in the Tower 16

Lost Explorers 18

History Raider! Hudson's Last Voyage 20

Mysterious Flight 22

History Raider! Amelia's Last Flight 24

Ongoing Mysteries 26

Mystery Solved? 28

Glossary 30

Learning More 31

Index 32

About the Author 32

VANISHING ACTS

History is brimming with unsolved disappearances. Some of these involve mighty rulers, daring adventurers, or royal families. Centuries later, the stories of these missing people still fascinate others.

Where Did They Go?

People have vanished under many puzzling circumstances. Some boarded ships or airplanes but never reached their destinations. **Records** were sometimes lost or destroyed on purpose, so people's whereabouts could not be found. Other people were presumed dead, but their bodies were never found. The mysteries surrounding these disappearances have never been solved. In some cases, people may have continued living, but with another identity. In other cases, their bodies may lie under the sea or inside an ancient, unknown **tomb**.

Looking for Answers

Today, if people disappear, there are many different ways to find them. Modern technologies and **DNA** testing can help track and identify them. However, disappearances in the past were much more difficult to solve. So we can turn to **evidence** to understand how people could simply vanish. **Archaeologists** and **historians** use the evidence to help build a story that may hold the key to some of history's most puzzling disappearances.

Many people, from archaeologists to **forensic** scientists, help investigate disappearances.

Stories of mysterious, abandoned ships are intriguing. One of the most famous is the story of the *Mary Celeste*, which set sail in 1872 with 10 people on board. Almost a month later, she was found abandoned but undamaged. All of her cargo was there, but none of the crew or passengers were found.

Explore History

In this book, we will journey across the world to discover the stories behind the most mysterious disappearances. As we do so, we will examine questions about the disappearances and gather evidence to try to answer them.

History Raider!

Hey! I'm Madison Maverick. I'm an explorer. I also like to think of myself as a history raider—a person who stops at nothing to find answers about the past. Come with me on my journeys to solve past mysteries and answer questions about history. Read my field notes on the History Raider pages and boxes. Then, jot down evidence to help solve each mystery.

LOST IN ANCIENT EGYPT

Thousands of years ago, women in Egypt held positions of great power. Many were queens who played a vital, but sometimes silent, role in ruling alongside their husbands. However, some of these female rulers seem to have vanished from historical records, and little is known about them. How has this happened?

The Queen Who Was King

Hatshepsut ruled ancient Egypt from about 1473 to 1458 B.C.E. She increased Egypt's **trade** with other kingdoms and ordered great building projects, such as the magnificent temple Deir el-Bahri. But after Hatshepsut died, her stepson Thutmose III took her name off the list of Egypt's pharaohs. He tore down statues and monuments that honored her. As a result, no one knew anything about Hatshepsut's story. Then, in 1822, archaeologists found and decoded **hieroglyphs** on the wall of Deir el-Bahri to learn about her. One interesting fact that was discovered was that in many places she was shown ruling as a male with muscles and a beard.

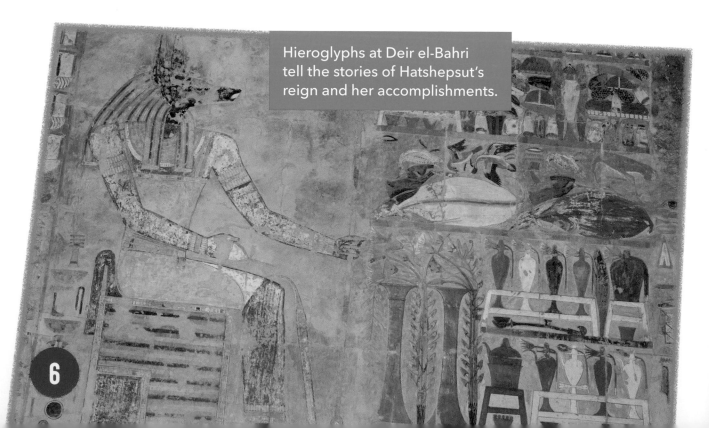

Hieroglyphs at Deir el-Bahri tell the stories of Hatshepsut's reign and her accomplishments.

Hidden from History

More than a century after Hatshepsut lived, Nefertiti was the Great Royal Wife to the pharaoh Akhenaton. However, Nefertiti seemed to vanish sometime in Akhenaton's twelfth year as king. She was mentioned only once in an **inscription** from the pharaoh's sixteenth year of reign. Other inscriptions suggest that Akhenaton had a joint ruler in the last years of his reign, which some believe might have been Nefertiti. After Akhenaton died, another leader took over until the **heir**, Tutankhamen, was old enough to rule. This ruler may also have been Nefertiti. The tomb of Nefertiti has never been found. Historians are still trying to locate the resting place of this mysterious queen.

Many images of Nefertiti decorate the temples of Akhenaton's reign. Her name means "the beautiful one is here."

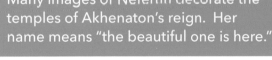

After reading about Nefertiti, I couldn't wait to dig into her story. Was she Akhenaton's joint ruler? Had she been Egypt's leader after his death? Are there any clues about where the body of this mystery queen might lie?

History Raider!
The Lost Queen

When I arrived in Egypt, I met an archaeologist who took me to the ruins of the ancient city of Amarna. This was where Nefertiti was last seen. If the rumors were true, Nefertiti may have ruled on her own after her husband died. There would be **artifacts** to support this idea.

A Favorite Queen

The archaeologists were still **excavating** Amarna when I visited, but they told me a lot. I learned that Nefertiti's husband Akhenaton built Amarna as Egypt's new capital. He created a whole religion around the sun god Aten. Nefertiti was the most important woman in the royal household. I studied pictures of artifacts that were uncovered in Amarna's ruins. Hieroglyphs showed Nefertiti as a powerful partner to her husband. She was shown leading the worship of Aten and driving a **chariot**. These were not things that queens normally did.

This **bust** of Nefertiti was sculpted around 1340 B.C.E. while she was queen at Amarna. It lay buried with other artifacts until its discovery in 1912.

8

Taking Charge

Cartouches mention a person called Neferneferuaten was a joint ruler with Akhenaton. Neferneferuaten was part of Nefertiti's full name. It's likely that Nefertiti used "Neferneferuaten" as a new title, and she was the joint ruler mentioned. The name "Smenkhkare" then appears as the new pharaoh after Akhenaton's death. Strangely, Smenkhkare had the same coronation name as Neferneferuaten. A coronation name is given to a ruler at the coronation ceremony. Since rulers did not share coronation names, it is reasonable to think that Nefertiti/Neferneferuaten and Smenkhkare are the same person. She became pharaoh on her own after Akhenaton's death.

The Missing Mummy

Nefertiti's body has never been found, even though Tutankhamen reburied royal mummies from Amarna in the Valley of the Kings in Egypt. Archaeologists used DNA testing to identify many of them, including Akhenaton. In 2020, archaeologists used **radar** at the tomb to discover that there were hidden chambers behind King Tutankhamen's burial chamber. Wouldn't it be amazing if they found Nefertiti there?

Finding Answers

Wow, can you believe that story? I think I figured out a lot about Nefertiti's last years and how important she may have been. What did you conclude after reading about this evidence? Turn to pages 28–29 to learn if your findings match mine.

A ROMAN MYSTERY

In 43 C.E., the Roman Emperor Claudius ordered four army legions, or units, to invade and take over Britain. When they arrived, the Romans encountered the **Celtic** Catuvellauni and Iceni tribes. The tribes fought fiercely, but they could not withstand the strength of the organized Roman forces. The Romans took control of much of the south. There was still fierce fighting in the north, however, and an entire Roman legion disappeared.

Roman Special Forces

The Legio IX Hispana, or the Spanish Ninth Legion, was one of Rome's most skilled groups of fighters. They battled against the Spanish and the fearsome Gauls in France. Then they moved into Britain and helped defeat the Catuvellauni people there. But in 60 or 61 C.E., Boudicca, the Celtic queen, led an army of Iceni to defeat the Ninth Legion. Boudicca's army also burned the Roman cities of London, St. Albans, and Colchester. This was a great victory for the tribes. However, it did not force the Romans to leave. They took control and lived there for around another 350 years.

Fighters of the Ninth Legion engraved their symbol on the fortresses they built. The Roman numerals "IX" mean nine.

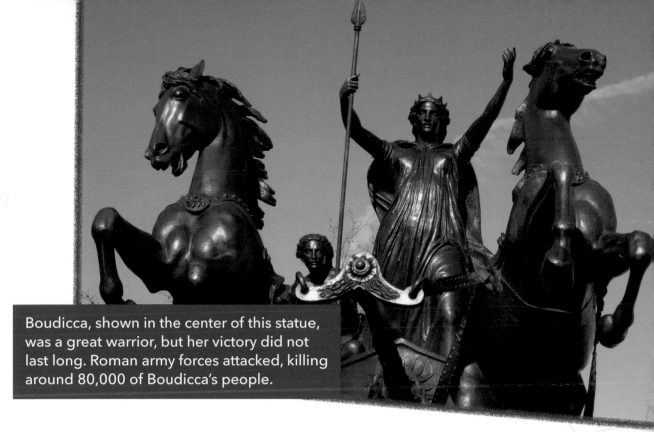

Boudicca, shown in the center of this statue, was a great warrior, but her victory did not last long. Roman army forces attacked, killing around 80,000 of Boudicca's people.

The Missing Army

After Boudicca wiped out so much of the Ninth Legion, Rome sent replacement soldiers to rebuild and strengthen their forces. The legion moved north over the next decades. It took over places such as York in England. At the time, York was a **strategic** point from which to launch the Roman assault on Caledonia, which is now Scotland. Then, somewhere between 108 and 120 C.E., the legion seemed to disappear without a trace.

History Raider!

It seemed crazy that 5,000 men could simply disappear! Did Caledonian soldiers kill and bury them all? Did the Roman emperor order the Ninth Legion to leave Britain? There's only one way to find out. I'm going to follow in their footsteps and see what I can discover.

History Raider!
Rome's Lost Legion

It was a little eerie wandering around the Roman ruins near York. I read that the soldiers of the Ninth Legion built their fortress here, but the ruins are all that is left of their time in Britain. Did they survive the battles with the Caledonians and go off to fight somewhere else? I hoped I could find some answers.

The Last Inscription

The last-known mention of the Ninth Legion in England was on a piece of stone from one of the main gates of the old Roman fort. It confirmed that the Ninth Legion was in York in 108 C.E. I wanted to find out what the Legion was doing before this time, so I read about the Roman **campaign** in Britain. I discovered that the Ninth Legion often fought with the fierce Caledonians. In 84 C.E., the Romans had their greatest victory. However, the Caledonians did not give up. According to historians, Rome lost many soldiers in Britain, especially during Roman emperor Hadrian's reign (117 to 138 C.E.). I was intrigued. Maybe the entire Ninth Legion was among these many deaths?

Emperor Hadrian ordered his soldiers to build a 73-mile (117-km) wall to protect Roman territory in Britain. Some of the wall still stands today.

Roman Cover-Up?

I discovered that there are no other records of the Ninth Legion after York in 108 C.E. In 165 C.E., Rome's Emperor Marcus Aurelius created a list of every Roman legion and its whereabouts. The Ninth Legion was not on his list! Had the Romans erased them from their records to hide the fact that the legion had been destroyed by the Caledonians?

Lost Soldiers

As I did a little more digging, I learned that over the centuries, no one has found any evidence of the Ninth Legion in Scotland. I began to wonder if perhaps the soldiers had left Britain. I found a news report about pieces of tile found in the Netherlands. The pieces bore the mark of the Ninth Legion. The tile pieces may have been left there around 121 C.E. Could the Ninth Legion have survived some of the battles in Britain and moved to the Netherlands? It seems that there may be more than one story behind this mysterious disappearance.

Finding Answers

The mystery of the disappearance of the Ninth Legion is a tricky one, but it's really fascinating! I found some interesting evidence about this mysterious disappearance. Did you? Look at pages 28–29 to see if your findings match mine!

MEDIEVAL MURDER?

Life in medieval **England was harsh. Poor people spent their days working the land. Townspeople worked for little money. Meanwhile, kings fought for power. One of the deadliest clashes took place between two houses, or branches, of the English royal family. It led to 30 years of fighting and unsolved murders.**

Fighting for the Throne

In 1452, Henry VI, from the House of Lancaster, was king. But the House of York, another branch of the family, wanted the crown. When Henry VI became sick in 1453, Richard, the Duke of York, became a temporary ruler as Protector of the Crown. He was promised that he would be the next king. However, the Lancasters did not want him to be king. When Henry VI recovered, Richard was removed from power.

Edward Takes Control

Richard fought for the crown, but was killed at the Battle of Wakefield in 1461. After his death, Richard's eldest son, Edward, gathered an army and defeated the Lancasters. He became King Edward IV. In 1465, Edward IV imprisoned Henry VI in the Tower of London. However, a battle led to Henry's release. Edward fled, but returned in 1471. He led the York forces to destroy the Lancaster army. Henry VI's son died in the battle. Since the crown was usually passed to the king's son, the way was clear for Edward to be king. Edward sent Henry VI back to the Tower, where he died under suspicious circumstances.

Richard, Duke of York (right), controlled England for a year after Henry VI became sick. Years of conflict, known as the Wars of the Roses, followed as both houses fought for the throne.

The Tower

Since it was built in 1070 C.E., England's kings and queens have used the Tower of London as a home, a place to store valuables, and a place to hide in times of trouble. They have also used it as a prison and a place of **execution**.

In April 1483, when Edward IV was dying, he asked his brother Richard, Duke of Gloucester, to protect his son, Prince Edward. Edward was heir to the throne. The Duke of Gloucester had other plans. He wanted to be king. After Edward died, the Duke sent his nephew to the Tower and took the crown for himself. Not long afterward, he sent his other nephew, Richard, to the Tower with Edward. The young boys soon vanished and were not seen again.

The last report of the princes at the Tower stated that they were seen playing on June 16, 1483.

History Raider!

The Tower of London seemed like such a scary place! The young princes must have been so frightened. What happened to them? Have their **remains** ever been found? I'm determined to find out.

History Raider!
Princes in the Tower

I knew that the Tower of London no longer held prisoners, but it was still a creepy place. On a tour, I visited the Bloody Tower. That is the part of the Tower of London where the princes may have stayed in the spring and summer of 1483. There, I read all about their story.

A Royal Murder?

Edward was 12 and Richard just 9 years old when their uncle sent them to the Tower. Once there, the Duke of Gloucester declared that the boys' parents were not legally married, so they had no right to the throne. He became King Richard III. That summer, there was just one sighting of the princes. Did Richard III kill the boys? Or did he have them sent away?

Gruesome Discovery

In 1674, workmen at the Tower uncovered two sets of bones buried in a box under a staircase. At the time, everyone believed the bones belonged to the two princes and that Richard III had killed them. However, other people could have wanted the princes to disappear. One of them was Henry Tudor, whose mother was part of the House of Lancaster. In 1485, Henry Tudor led a battle against Richard III. Richard died, and Henry became king.

Looking for Evidence

I kept reading and found out that scientists examined the bones in 1933. They wrote that the remains belonged to children of around the same ages as the princes—12 and 10 years old. But they did not know if they were boys' bones. There was no DNA testing or **radiocarbon dating** back then. I wondered if they could do the test now. Researchers found Richard III's remains in 2012 and identified them the next year. Scientists could see if those remains and the children's bones shared some DNA. That didn't happen, though, because the Church of England refused to release the children's bones. It looked like my investigation had gone cold.

ENTRY TO THE TRAITORS GATE

In 1493, an Italian guest at the English **court** wrote that the princes were moved from the Bloody Tower to the White Tower. The White Tower was the place for prisoners.

Finding Answers

I hope that, one day, DNA evidence can prove what happened to the princes. Until then, I found some intriguing clues about their disappearances. Do your findings match mine? Turn to pages 28-29 to find out.

LOST EXPLORERS

European explorers have crossed oceans, trekked through deserts, and braved frozen lands. They searched for riches, expanded empires, mapped lands, and studied plants and animals. Not all of these men and women returned from their journeys, however. Some were never seen again.

A Route East

In the early 1400s, Europeans wanted spices, silks, and jewels from East Asia. Middle Eastern traders controlled the transfer of these goods. When they blocked overland routes, Europeans looked for other ways eastward. At first, they sent ships around Africa and through the Indian Ocean. This took a long time. Europeans were frightened to travel across the Atlantic Ocean, which they called the Sea of Darkness. But they decided that it might be the fastest path to the East. They did not know that North America existed.

In the late 1400s, Christopher Columbus headed across the Atlantic hoping to find Asia. Instead, he sailed south to the Caribbean Islands. A few years later, Italian John Cabot went in search of the "Northwest Passage." Europeans believed that this was a route around the north end of America. If they could find it, the route could be the shortest sea route from the Atlantic to the Pacific Ocean. Cabot did not find it. He landed in what is now Eastern Canada. In 1498, Cabot made another trip, but he and his ship were never seen again.

A statue in Bristol, England, honors John Cabot. Cabot probably died at sea, but some stories suggest that he returned to England in 1500 and died there.

This 1860 illustration shows items found scattered in the western Arctic. They belonged to another lost explorer, Sir John Franklin.

Lost in the Ice

After Cabot, more explorers disappeared in the quest to find the Northwest Passage. In 1610, Henry Hudson and his crew traveled aboard the *Discovery* to the Canadian Arctic and into what is now Hudson Bay. Problems on board led to a **mutiny**. Most of the crew abandoned Hudson and a few other men, forcing them into a small ship. The crew sailed the *Discovery* back to England. Ever since, historians have been trying to piece together the clues about Hudson's disappearance.

History Raider!

The story of Henry Hudson was a tragic story that stirred my curiosity. Did the crew of the *Discovery* simply leave Hudson and the others, or did they murder them? Is there a chance that Hudson somehow survived? Maybe I'll find some answers in Canada.

19

History Raider!
Hudson's Last Voyage

I took a helicopter ride over Hudson Bay to see the spot where Henry Hudson's crew said they'd left him. It looked vast, icy, and far away from everything. There was nowhere to do my research, so my next stop was Ottawa.

Another Attempt

I found out that Hudson's son, John, had joined his father on their fateful 1610 voyage. On this journey, Hudson steered the *Discovery* south of Greenland and into a **strait** between Baffin Island and northern Quebec. From there, Hudson sailed south into a huge body of water. He thought he had entered the Pacific Ocean.

Trouble Aboard the Ship

Hudson sailed the ship along the eastern part of the bay. He realized that this was not the Pacific. He continued on to James Bay. The crew spent the winter there because Hudson wanted to continue exploring in the spring. According to the crew, Hudson was a harsh captain. The men believed that Hudson kept food from them and treated them unfairly. They were very unhappy. In June 1611, the crew organized a mutiny. They forced Hudson, his son, and seven other men into a small boat. Then the *Discovery* sailed away. Due to clashes with locals and scarce food, only eight of the crew survived the trip back to England. The survivors denied killing Hudson, and no one was punished.

Hudson could have navigated along inland rivers and encountered First Nations people. If so, did they kill him or allow him to live with them?

Survival Stories

Did Hudson and the other men die in the small boat? Were they murdered by the crew? Or, could they have found land and survived among the **First Nations** people who lived in the area? A few years after Hudson's disappearance, there was a report that a young Englishman was living among the Anishinaabe people. Could this man have been Hudson? Hundreds of years later, in 1959, a road crew found a stone northwest of Ottawa. Inscribed in the stone was: HH 1612 CAPTIVE. Were Hudson and his son captured, and by whom? Despite searching, historians have never found any further evidence.

Finding Answers

That was a fascinating trip! There are some different clues about Hudson's disappearance. What information did you write down? Turn to pages 28–29 to see if your notes match mine.

MYSTERIOUS FLIGHT

Airplanes are huge, powerful vehicles. It seems impossible that any could disappear without a trace. Still, a number of flights, their pilots, and their passengers have done just that. Did the missing planes change course? Did they crash into water? Only proven evidence can help solve these mysteries.

Flying off the Radar

Malaysian Airlines flight 370 took off after midnight on March 8, 2014, from Kuala Lumpur, Malaysia. It was carrying 12 crew and 227 passengers. The plane was supposed to fly to Beijing, China. The last communication with the plane was at 1:19 a.m. Radar tracked the plane as it turned around and flew in the opposite direction. The last signals came in at 8:11 a.m. over the Indian Ocean—in the opposite direction of its destination. Searches lasting more than a year found just 27 pieces of debris washed up on the shores of different African countries. Today, no one knows why the flight went off course, or where it crashed or landed.

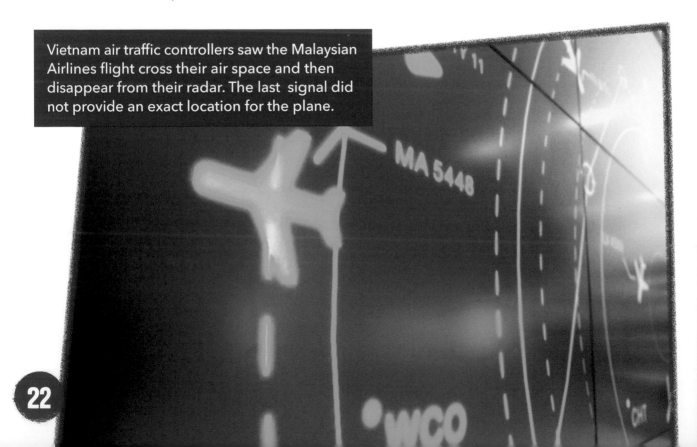

Vietnam air traffic controllers saw the Malaysian Airlines flight cross their air space and then disappear from their radar. The last signal did not provide an exact location for the plane.

In 1937, radios picked up distress signals coming from an area that included Nikumaroro, a western Pacific island. Did Earhart and Noonan send the signal?

Lost in the Pacific

In the 1930s, Amelia Earhart was famous for being the first female pilot to fly solo across the Atlantic Ocean and the first woman to fly solo across the United States. Her goal was to fly around the world. On June 1, 1937, Earhart and her navigator, Fred Noonan, set off from Miami, Florida, in a small Lockheed Electra plane. They flew toward South America and then went east across the Atlantic and Indian Oceans. On June 29, their plane landed in New Guinea, an island in the western Pacific Ocean. Earhart and Noonan left there on July 2, heading for a stop at Howland Island, 2,500 miles (4,023 km) away. They never arrived.

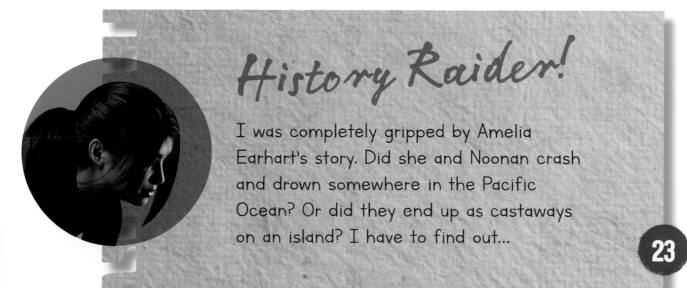

History Raider!

I was completely gripped by Amelia Earhart's story. Did she and Noonan crash and drown somewhere in the Pacific Ocean? Or did they end up as castaways on an island? I have to find out...

23

History Raider!
Amelia's Last Flight

I began my research by looking at a map showing the Phoenix Islands. Investigators think Earhart and Noonan landed on or near Nikumaroro. Since 1989, The International Group for Historic Aircraft Recovery (TIGHAR) has conducted the Amelia Earhart Project. They've carried out 12 expeditions to Nikumaroro and collected a ton of research.

The First Searches

When Earhart and Noonan failed to arrive at Howland Island, the U.S. Navy and Coast Guard searched for two weeks. They covered around 250,000 square miles (647,497 sq km). The Navy concluded that the Electra had run out of fuel and crashed into the Pacific. What they didn't consider at the time was a detail about Nikumaroro. On July 9, 1937, the Navy reported signs of life on the island, but they did not think this was significant. They did not know that no one had lived there since 1892.

Scraps of Evidence

In 1991, TIGHAR's researchers at Nikumaroro found a piece of aluminum with rivets, or bolts. They believed it came from the Electra. They also found a broken bottle and a jar. Both would have been made around Earhart's time. Scientists examined the jar and reported that it had held face cream. I was getting excited by what I was discovering. Did this prove that Amelia Earhart had lived on Nikumaroro?

A Blurry Photograph

In 2019, Dr. Robert Ballard led another major search around Nikumaroro. He was intrigued by a very blurry picture TIGHAR had in evidence. It was taken near Nikumaroro in 1937 and seemed to show a piece of the Electra's landing gear. Bones were also found on Nikumaroro in 1940. At the time, the analysis showed the bones belonged to a man. In 1998, however, TIGHAR tracked down the analysis. An **anthropologist** concluded that the bones were likely female and the right height for Earhart.

Studies of the Electra found that the plane would have carried enough fuel to reach Nikumaroro. The team at TIGHAR believe that Earhart landed safely but that Noonan was injured and died.

The Search Goes On

Dr. Ballard found nothing of the Electra or any other evidence linked to Earhart. But archaeologists took some soil samples where the bones were found. They also took a female skull found at a museum on a nearby island. Scientists plan to look for DNA to match to one of Earhart's living relatives.

Finding Answers

What a mind-blowing mission! I found some convincing evidence that helped answer some of my questions! Did you? Turn to pages 28–29 to see if your notes match mine.

ONGOING MYSTERIES

Today, the Internet and social media make the search for missing people easier. Most people leave some kind of digital footprint or other evidence of their identity online. New techniques and computer technologies also help track down missing people today.

Fingerprint Dating

Since the late 1800s, investigators have dusted for fingerprints to place people at a certain location or prove they touched a certain object. New equipment goes even further. Scientists have developed tests to determine what day the fingerprints were left. They determine the date by looking at how the oils from the print have faded over time. Unfortunately, the test only works for newer prints, so it will not help solve any disappearances from long ago.

Underwater Search

Sonar and radar equipment are very accurate in finding things lost underwater. Sonar can detect objects below the water's surface. Automated Underwater Vehicles (AUVs) are robot detectives. They have cameras and **sensors** that can take photos and detect things, even deep underwater. Water wears away evidence, but new technologies may help identify remains that cannot be seen with the naked eye.

It is dangerous for people to dive too deep in the ocean. AUVs can do the work instead. They can collect information from the ocean floor.

Eyes in the Sky

Tracking technology using GPS can be installed on cell phones, in jewelry, and on cars. It makes it much easier to find out where people go. Remotely piloted aircraft systems (RPAS) use cameras and thermal, or heat, imaging sensors. These sensors recognize people and shapes.

Artificial intelligence (AI) uses facial recognition technology to find missing people. In China, a two-year-old boy was kidnapped in 1988. Police scientists aged a photo of the boy to see what he would look like today. The facial recognition technology scanned the photo and found a match in its database, or store of information. The parents were reunited with their lost son after 32 years.

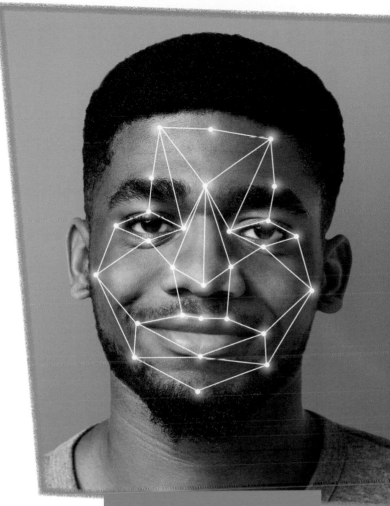

A facial recognition system maps features from a photograph. The system then matches the features to information it has stored.

History Raider!

For adventurers like us, the world is full of mysteries and wonders to explore. The history of mysterious disappearances has been so much fun to explore. I can hardly wait to investigate disappearances in the future.

27

MYSTERY SOLVED?

Some of the disappearances were really puzzling, weren't they? After gathering evidence, here are some conclusions I made after each journey. How do yours match up?

Pages 8-9: The Lost Queen

Nefertiti is likely to have been a joint ruler with Akhenaton. Artifacts show that Nefertiti was a powerful woman. Neferneferuaten, the name of the joint ruler with Akhenaton, was part of Nefertiti's full name. The hidden chambers at Tutankhamen's tomb may be the final resting place of Nefertiti.

Pages 12-13: Rome's Lost Legion

It seems likely that the Roman legion was wiped out in battle by the Caledonians. The Romans may have covered up their defeat by choosing not to list the legion in 165 C.E. However, a tile bearing the legion's mark was found in the Netherlands. It is therefore possible that the Ninth Legion may have left Britain for the Netherlands.

Pages 16-17: Princes in the Tower

It is likely that the boys died in the Tower. Tests on the bones found there showed that they belonged to children ages 12 and 10. Without DNA analysis, it cannot be proven that these are the bones of the princes, but it seems likely.

Pages 20-21:
Hudson's Last Voyage

It is very possible that Hudson and his loyal men died on the small boat or were murdered by the *Discovery* crew. However, reports after Hudson's disappearance stated that a young Englishman was living among the Anishinaabe. A stone found in 1959 with the inscription "HH 1612 CAPTIVE" suggests a different fate: that Hudson was kidnapped.

Pages 24-25:
Amelia's Last Flight

Although the Navy assumed the Electra had run out of fuel and crashed in the Pacific, there was a lot of evidence to suggest otherwise. On July 9, 1937, a flyover of Nikumaroro noted signs of life. No one had lived there since 1892. On Nikumaroro, TIGHAR found a piece of aluminum possibly from the Electra. TIGHAR also found a jar dated to the 1930s. Bones found were female and matched Earhart's height. All this evidence suggests that Amelia may have survived the flight and lived on Nikumaroro for an undetermined amount of time.

GLOSSARY

anthropologist A scientist who studies human societies and cultures

archaeologists People who study history through artifacts and remains

artifacts Objects that were made by people in the past

bust A sculpture of a person's head

campaign In military terms, a series of battles and attacks

cartouches Ovals enclosing a group of hieroglyphs, usually showing a name

Celtic Relates to the Celts: a group of people who lived from what is now Turkey in the east to the British Isles and northern Spain in the west

chariot A two-wheeled carriage that was pulled by horses and used in battle in ancient times

court An extended royal household, including those who often visit the ruler and guests

DNA The substance in cells that carries unique information about living things

evidence A sign that shows that something exists or is true

excavating Digging into the earth to uncover things

execution Killing someone

First Nations Groups of Indigenous peoples in Canada who were first to inhabit the land

forensic Relating to scientific methods used to solve crimes or past events

heir Next in line to be king or queen

hieroglyphs Ancient Egyptian writing that used pictures instead of letters

historians People who study history

inscription Something written onto a monument

medieval Describes the time between 500 and 1500 C.E.

mutiny A rebellion, especially by sailors or soldiers, against their leaders

radar A system that uses radio waves to locate objects

radiocarbon dating Dating objects by measuring the carbon in them

records Official documents of events

remains Pieces or parts left over

sensors Devices that detect things and transmit the data to a computer

sonar A system using sound waves to detect objects in water

strait A passage of water that connects two larger bodies of water

strategic Describes plans to bring about a specific outcome

tomb A building where a corpse is kept

trade The buying and selling of goods

LEARNING MORE

BOOKS

Dakers, Diane. *Amelia Earhart: Pioneering Aviator and Force for Women's Rights* (Crabtree Groundbreaker Biographies). Crabtree Publishing, 2016.

George, Enzo. *Mysterious Disappearances* (The Paranormal Throughout History). Rosen, 2020.

Guiberson, Brenda Z. *Missing: Mysterious Cases of People Gone Missing Through the Centuries*. Henry Holt, 2019.

MacLeod, Elizabeth. *Vanished: True Tales of Mysterious Disappearances*. Annick Press, 2016.

WEBSITES

Read stories of other mysterious disappearances at:
www.britannica.com/list/9-mysterious-disappearances-of-people-other-than-amelia-earhart

Learn facts about Amelia Earhart and her disappearance at:
www.childrensmuseum.org/blog/10-facts-about-amelia-earhart

Find out more about the story of Henry Hudson and his explorations at:
www.thecanadianencyclopedia.ca/en/article/henry-hudson

Read more about the English princes in the Tower of London at:
https://kids.kiddle.co/Edward_V_of_England

INDEX

Akhenaton 7, 8, 9, 28
Anishinaabe people 21, 29
archaeologists 4, 6, 8, 9, 25
artifacts 8, 28
artificial intelligence (AI) 27
AUVs 26

Boudicca 10, 11

Cabot, John 18, 19
Caledonians 11, 12, 13, 28
cartouches 9

Discovery 16, 19, 20, 29
DNA testing 4, 9, 17

Earhart, Amelia 23, 24, 25, 29
Edward IV 14, 15, 17
Electra 23, 24, 25, 29
European explorers 18

facial recognition system 27
fingerprint dating 26
First Nations 21

forensic scientists 4

Hatshepsut 6, 7
hieroglyphs 6, 8
Hudson, Henry 19, 20

Malaysian Airlines flight 370 22
Mary Celeste 5
mutiny 19, 20

Nefertiti 7, 8, 9, 28
Nikumaroro 23, 24, 25, 29
Ninth Legion 10, 11, 12, 13, 28
Northwest Passage 18, 19

Princes in the Tower 15, 16, 28

radar 9, 22, 26
radiocarbon dating 17
Richard III 16, 17

TIGHAR 24, 25, 29
Tower (of London) 14, 15, 16, 28
Tutankhamen 7, 9, 28

About the Author

Cynthia O'Brien has written many books for children, including those about science and history. Researching this book, she learned a lot about strange disappearances that happened in the past and how people, and even whole civilizations, just vanished. Some of the disappearances sent chills down her spine!